Bowly Can Take Big, Calm, Melting Breaths

A Self-Regulation Story
by Angharad Davies

The Positive
Motherhood Project

First published in 2024 by The Positive Motherhood Project Ltd

www.bowlycan.com

© 2024 Angharad Davies

ISBN: 978-1-7390947-1-3

For my six-year-old Owen,
the talented budding illustrator.
The teddy was all him!

Hello there!

I can't seem to find my friend.
His name's Bowly McLight.
He's a little light-filled bowl.
We were supposed to meet up here.

Hold on.
What's all this mud?
I wonder...

Here you are, Bowly.
You're covered head to toe in mud.
I can see you're feeling frustrated.

Is that a stone I can see in there,
blocking all your light?
A stone sometimes comes when
you're feeling frustrated, doesn't it?

I bet you want to get that stone
out and let your light shine again.

YEAH.

Oh, you've taken out your stone
and you've closed your eyes, Bowly.

As big as an eight.

Ah, that's how frustrating it feels to be covered in mud right now. And I can see you're taking some slow, deep breaths.

Wow, the stone is melting.
The frustration must be feeling smaller.

As big as
a four.

You're taking more deep breaths.

The stone has completely melted.
The frustration has gone.

As small
as a one.

Bowly, open your eyes.
Look!

Waaah!!!

WET FEET!
BOOTS! BOOTS!!

Good idea, Bowly.
Some boots will do the trick.

Oh, but they seem tough to get on.
I can see that you're feeling frustrated, Bowly.
You've got a stone in there blocking out
your light again.

You've taken out your stone and closed your eyes again, Bowly. And you're taking slow, deep breaths.

As big as
a nine.

That's how frustrating it feels
trying to put on your boots.
That is a big number. I can see
why your stone was so big this time.

The stone is melting.
You're feeling less frustrated, Bowly.
You're still taking big, slow breaths.

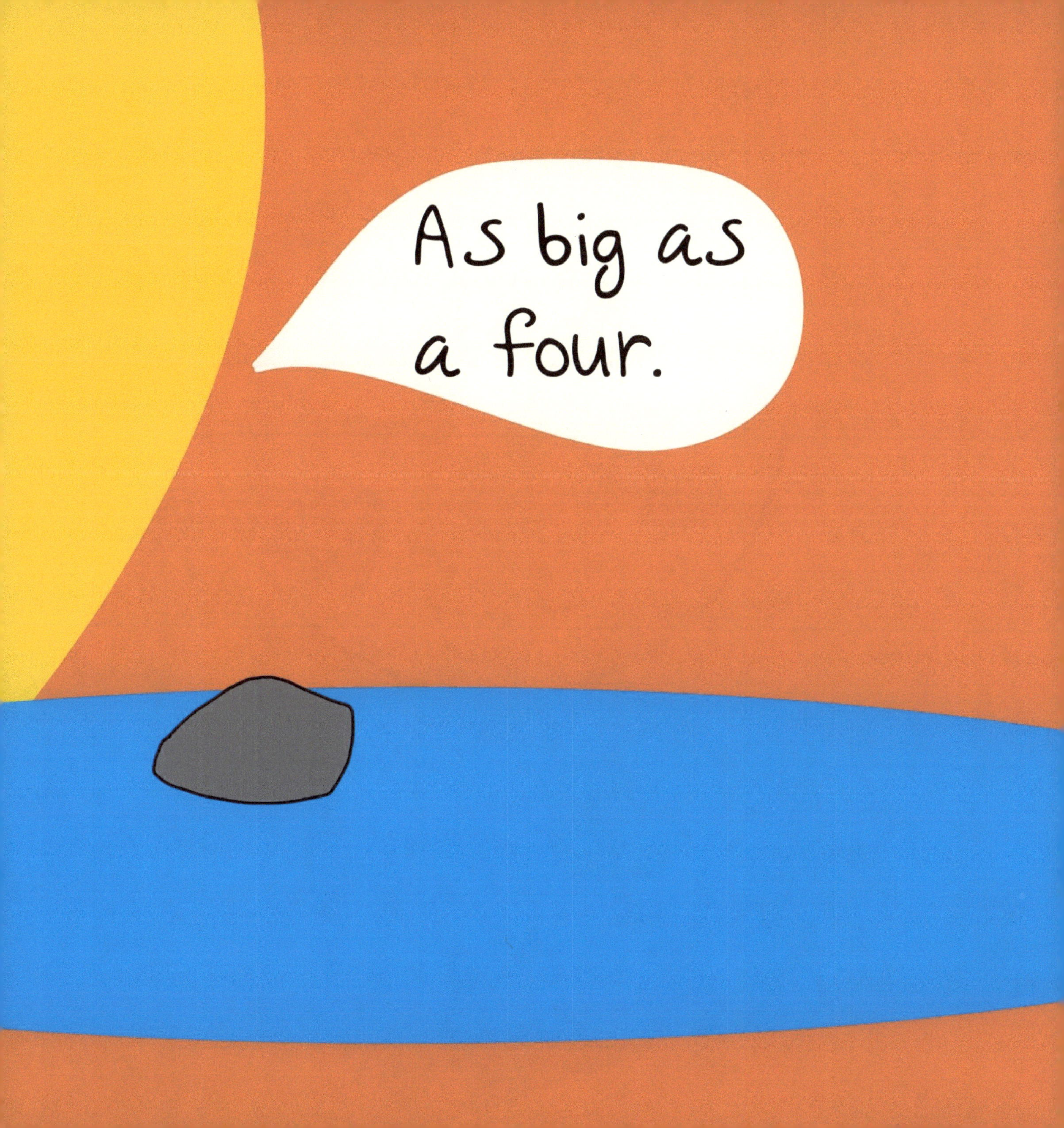
As big as a four.

The stone has completely melted.
The frustration has gone.

As small as a one.

Bowly, open your eyes.
Look!

More water?
TO THE RESCUE!
RAH!

Oh my, Bowly!
Where are you going?
What's going on?

Oh no, teddy is all wet.
That boat is a good idea, Bowly.
Teddy will stay dry on there.

Oh no, teddy keeps falling off the boat.
I can see you're feeling angry.
And an even bigger stone is blocking your light now.

As small
as a one.

Oh my, Bowly.
Your stone has totally melted.
Your anger has completely gone.
But maybe you shouldn't open your eyes.

The story might be over, but Bowly has one last thing for you.

Make Bowly's tool come alive in the FREE video training

Take your very own Bowly with you wherever you go! Learn how to use the big, calm, melting breath at home, at school and out and about.

If Bowly can...

... so can you!

www.bowlycan.com/f/melt

The transportable Bowly-in-the-hand move will be a game-changer for your child!
Easy and practical to use, before long your little one will be reminding you to use the big, calm, melting breath!

About the author

Angharad Davies lives in the UK with her ever-so-supportive husband and her two amazing little boys.

After witnessing the magic of story in her own children for nurturing emotional intelligence and resilience, she decided to write her own.

Combining her knowledge from postgraduate qualifications in Psychology and Play Therapy with her children's love for humorous reads, Bowly McLight was born. With the help of her own children's story ideas and illustrations, Angharad is on a mission to deliver practical mindset and resilience tools to children through the power of story.

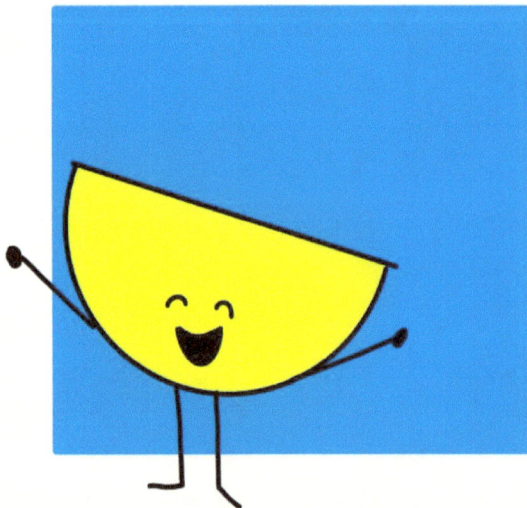

About Bowly

Bowly was inspired by the Hawaiian teaching of the Bowl of Light.

He is fun-loving and adores a challenge. He wears his big emotions on his sleeve and is on a mission to teach children everywhere the coolest of tools, so that they too can face anything life throws at them - even big dragons!

A new tool in every story

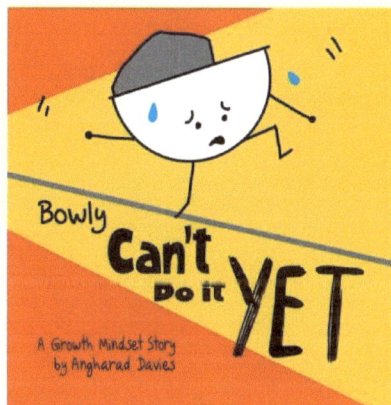

Bowly is feeling frustrated and is ready to give up learning to walk the tightrope when a mysterious word appears. Where did it come from and can it help Bowly to keep going?

A charming story to introduce children to the power of *yet* and learning to persevere when things get tough.
The perfect book for helping children to build resilience and growth mindset.

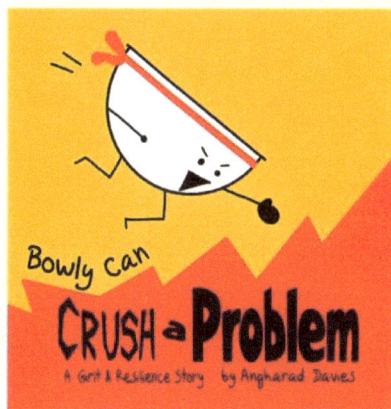

Bowly faces challenge after challenge, but never gives up. He has a karate-chopping-problem-solving trick up his sleeve! There's nothing that can stop him, except a dragon maybe.

A super fun story to teach children a powerful question when faced with a problem: *"What's the hard part?"*
The perfect book to help nurture resilience and a solution-focused mindset.

9 781739 094713